Word Love
The Rise and Fall of a Blog

Elizabeth Gross

ISBN: 1517024366
ISBN-13: 978-1517024369

DEDICATION

To my cheering section and support team:
Judi, Frank, Susi, Megan, and Jill

Introduction

A while ago I wrote a blog about words - the meaning and cultural aspects of words. Each post was a different subject. A lot of the content was taken from my own life. It was an exercise in writing to amuse.

Along the way I went through several stages of authorship. The exhilaration of creating. The joy of being disciplined enough to write every day. The tedium of writing every day. The realization that you don't need to write every day. The boredom of blogging when no one reads it. And finally, the realization that I could quit without losing my dignity.

So I quit. And in quitting, I explored the reasons why it was not successful. And I took some time to analyze them and write them out hoping that they will help some future blogger. This book is a journey through the creative method, along with my thought processes in starting and ending the blog.

6

MY STORY

I was one of those kids who loved phonics. Sounding out words was fun for me. (I still like to look at a name and figure out how to pronounce it.) My main interests became reading and writing. Mostly reading up until a few years ago. That's when I decided to start a home-based business.

I researched it a bit and found that I should ask myself this question: "What to you like to do?" "Well," I said to myself, "I like to read. And write. And web surf." "OK," myself replied.

"Can you make money doing that?" "I don't know", I said.

"Let's find out!"

Yes. I am hokey. And if you don't know what that word means, stay tuned. It'll come up later.

So I started a business doing internet research and computer instruction. Taught a few classes. Had a few customers. But I wasn't doing very well.

"No motivation," myself whispers. ("Shut up," I say.)

Elizabeth Gross

So I did some more self-research, and decided that writing was what I enjoyed most. Content writing became my new modus operandi.

Resulting in this a business called EJG Research. EJG is me. I kept the research part because that's what I do to find what to write. And all the cool names with the word "write" in them seem to be taken. And no, I won't tell you my middle name unless you buy me dinner.

So here on this blog, I will attempt to show you how much I love words. And some of the other pages will help you hire me as a content writer/researcher. You'll find lots of information, when I actually write those other pages, like contact details, and mission statement, pricing data, and yada, yada, yada…is there a copyright on that term?

In the meantime….

This blog will be a compilation of words. What they mean. How they are used. The history of the word. Maybe even a definition.

One word per post. Maybe one per day. Maybe two. Maybe three or four a week. But I do promise to keep blogging until you all get sick of me. Or my fingers cramp. Whichever comes first.

So this is how I started out. A bit lame, I admit, but it was my voice. All the blogging experts said "Find your authentic voice." And yes, this was mine.

Since I had started a home-based business about research and content writing, I thought a good idea to promote it would be to write a blog about the very thing I was using as the major component of my services – words.

One of the major rules of marketing is "Know your competition!" The writing sources all said find a niche - a need that no one else is filling. So I looked around the web to see what kind of competition I would have. Luckily, there was not much. There were hundreds of blogs about writing, but very few about words themselves. This seemed to be a good sign. I believed I had found an untapped niche.

Lesson learned #1

A dearth of content about a subject sometimes means no one cares about that subject.

I spent a lot of time looking up information on How To Write A Blog. I used search terms like writing a blog, about blogging, and even blogs about blogs. I began to feel like there is an overabundance of information on how to write.

After satisfying my craving for research on this particular topic, I sat down and created a WordPress blog. The first entry went like this…

Elizabeth Gross

WORD LOVE

People have asked me why, at the age of 59, did I decide to start a second career of freelance writing. Basically, the answer is, so that my retirement doesn't end up being dollar microwave meals and second-hand magazines.

A few years ago, I finally sat down and looked at my retirement reality. I saw that I was indeed one of those stupid baby boomers who had not saved for my "golden years" the way I should have.

So, I thought up Plan A and Plan B.

Plan A was: find a rich man to marry.

So I went with Plan B: get a second income.

Word Love

Some of you know I have had some past home businesses that didn't really work out. The latest one, internet research, was probably doable, but I discovered I enjoyed writing the reports a lot more than I thought I would.

Writing has always been my "goto dream" when asked what my life dream was. But circumstances got in the way, and it never happened.

Until now. I looked at some side businesses, (cause I sure ain't gonna quit my day job!) and saw freelance writing mentioned over and over. Huh, I thought. I can write. I like to write. I can make money writing? WHY AM I NOT WRITING!

So I formed this final (I think) home-based business of doing freelance writing and internet research. Cause, ya know, I do love researching and it goes with the territory.

Yes, there's that same lame "authentic voice." I thought some humor would bring in the crowds.

Lesson learned #2

Don't be a comedian if you are not a professional comedian.

These first attempts at humor got zero comments. ZERO. I never have found out if anyone actually read them.

I dove right in anyway, writing posts. One thing I did take away from my research was that you need a picture with every post. It shows you gave some thought to the subject. Also, it looks really good when you post the blog entry on Facebook.

Finding graphics is easy. Finding copy write-free pictures is a bit harder. You can't just copy and paste any clip art you see. There are rules. There are legal ramifications. There could be fines and punishment. Choosing a picture that was created by someone else is not okay if it has a copyright. Selecting a graphic from Creative Commons, or a "free to use" list is fine.

My advice to you is to look up and understand the Digital Millennium Copyright Act (DMCA). Please be careful when you choose a picture.

Satisfied?

Satisfaction. Now there's a comforting word. To satisfy –
fulfill the desires, needs, wants of … someone, or
something. Your mate, your stomach, your wanderlust.

All kinds of things are satisfying. A job well done. A really
good book. A delicious meal. A well-brought up child.
Chocolate.

Satisfaction is that knowledge that you have succeeded. In a
career. In an educational endeavor. In a quest for the
perfect thing. You have "made it." You have reached the
pinnacle. You have arrived.

Satisfaction can be a dangerous thing, as well. You can be
satisfied with the status quo and never do what you are
really meant to do. You can be satisfied with your personal
relationships and never move on when it's obvious you need

to. You can be satisfied with "the way things are" and never try to change.

Be careful when you have reached a state of satisfaction. A quick emotion check may bring up some alternative ideas of what your life might be like if you decide to be dissatisfied with the way things are.

I feel satisfied that I have really begun to create this startup business. I've finally taken that step, the one that scared me for so long. It truly is satisfying. What are you satisfied with? And is it a good feeling..or do you think you should revisit your reasoning?

See how I ended it with a question? All the experts say "End your post with a question and people will write comments. Then you can form a relationship with them."

Lesson learned #3

A question does not guarantee any comments.

This is something I struggled with on every post. Eventually I did get a few comments. The first one generated a feeling of accomplishment. However it quickly disappeared when the comments became very few and far between.

As far as the actual post goes. this first attempt was short and I felt to the point. I was so anxious to get something up on the site that I made the mistake of terseness. Looking back, it needs some depth. The format is not very good. In the next post I started using space to separate out the definition of the word.

Elizabeth Gross

Elegance…A Way to See the World

"Elegance is the only beauty that never fades."

~ Audrey Hepburn~

If something is elegant, what exactly does that mean? Beautiful? Refined? Sophisticated? Yes, all this, and more.

Elegance is defined as: (compliments of dictionary.com)

adjective

1.tastefully fine or luxurious in dress, style, design, etc.
2.gracefully refined and dignified, as in tastes, habits, or literary style
3.graceful in form or movement
4.appropriate to refined taste
5.excellent; fine; superior

Word Love

Well! Sounds quite la-de-da, doncha' think?

I don't. Elegance is something I believe everyone should strive for. It sets you apart from the riff-raff. If you want society in general to consider you a responsible adult, then acting in an unrefined, ungraceful, or tasteless manner will not endear you to many people.

The Simplicity of it all

Being elegant is not just looking like an early 1900's debutante. While it does give you a good excuse to dress "to the nines", it simply means good grooming, good hygiene, and good manners. Dress the part and the world will see you thus.

It also does not mean that you can use ignorance as an excuse. If you learn about the world around you, the ways of society, and the reasons for being a decent human being, you will become a bit more enlightened. Elegant people are intellectual and informed.

Some simple ways to portray the fact that you are indeed an elegant person are:

1. Using politeness – Please and thank you show others that you are a refined member of society

Elizabeth Gross

2. Being respectful – of everyone, even those you disagree with

3. Showing kindness to all – people and animals alike

4. Having a generous spirit – giving of yourself, your talents, your knowledge, and not just your money

Another Way to Look at it

The term elegant is also used in computer science, mathematics, and other sciences. It refers to a simple answer or solution. A consistency of color, or line, or technique. A theory is considered elegant if it offers a complete solution without an overwhelming amount of ideas.

Rather a good way to perceive the world.

Are you elegant? What makes you so? Post a comment.

Once again I used a question to generate comments. However, adding the command to "post a comment" pretty much makes me look like a desperate soul.

And, again, no comments.

Notice I used a quote-from-a-famous-person. Always a good way to catch attention. It's a method of SEO or Search Engine Optimization. When I began this project SEO was the thing considered to be the only way to get top listing in search engines. There are whole web sites dedicated to it. Lately I've read that it's waste of time. I'll leave an opinion up to you.

The next couple of posts show that I started to pick up some good habits. I began to give more credit to my research sources. I was using links to enhance the information.

Elizabeth Gross

Hooray! Hurrah! Huzzah!

Hurray! Way to go! Good Job! You did it! What a good feeling this sends. Everyone loves praise and Hurray! is the best. A cheer for your efforts.

Ever wonder where the word came from?

There is evidence it goes all the way back to the Crusades. "The saying "hip hip hurrah" is alleged to have roots going back to the crusaders, meaning "Jerusalem is lost to the infidel, and we are on our way to paradise". The abbreviation HEP would then stand for *Hierosolyma est perdita*, "Jerusalem is lost" in Latin." http://www.wikipwdia.org

There is also speculation that it came from sailors. I can see the significance of a good Huzza! after hoisting the sails on those clipper ships. Other sources may be the Norse warrior cry "Haer Av! translated as Heads off! Or perhaps the Mongol hordes yelling Huree! with the same meaning as Amen! or Hallelujah!

In more modern times, we hear it at football games, starting in the 1800's as Rah Rah Rah usually accompanied by Sis Boom Bah! It even occurs in British Parliament as the positive acknowledgement Hear! Hear!

At any rate, we commonly use Hooray or Hurrah for ordinary celebrations. Huzza is reserved for rowing crews and Renaissance Faires.

So, Hooray for Hollywood. or Hazel. or the Super Readers saving the day. What are your reasons for shouting Hooray? Let me know in the comments.

Elizabeth Gross

Weight – A Heavy Word Indeed

I weigh too much. Yeah, you're thinking, who doesn't? Well, a lot of people actually. My younger daughter's weight has been below 110 pounds all her life. (And this after 4 children)

Yet I can't loose any. Weight is an elusive thing. Lose it, gain it, but we're never satisfied.

The word has a certain mass appeal. (yeah that's a pun). Weighty subjects are discussed by serious students in college dorms, Weight-lifters are worshiped by preteen boys. It is thrown around by people wanting to show how important they are. Others pull their own to prove their worth. And some things carry it when they have significance.

As a measurement, weight proves how heavy or light something is. Unfortunately, some people use it as the only way to measure a person's worthiness. But please, don't judge by weight. Pounds don't matter. After all, an adult brain only weighs 3 pounds. But what a massive thing a mind can be.

So, are you enjoying this blog? Let me know what words you want discussed by filling out the poll here:

What kind of words peak your interest?

○ Trendy (pop culture, entertainment, etc.)

○ Academic (science, history, etc.)

○ In the news

○ Slang

VoteView ResultsPolldaddy.com

I guarantee every vote carries the same weight.

So by this time I was feeling the first twinges of discouragement. Still no feedback. I was still learning all I could as I went along. So I found a new idea to incorporate in my posts. A poll.

Wanting to gather ideas from my readers, I asked what words they wanted to know about.

Zero response.

Ah well. Onward!

It's Political

Beware. This post is a bit of a rant.

What a world! Chaos, anger, dissension, all around. And it's all political!

I 'm so tired of politics. What are they anyway? Let's see... according to .Dictionary.com, politics is:

◊ The science or art of political government.   Science? Art?

Aren't these things what some politicians are trying to get rid of?

◊ Political affairs   Well there certainly are a lot of those.

◊ Political methods or maneuvers.   Hmmm, maneuvers are like manipulations, right?

◊ Political principles or opinions   And where can we find the most opinionated people? Uh-huh.

Of course, there are politics everywhere, not just in government. School, office, even your home. Oh you don't think so? Who's the boss, really? (And yes, the baby is eligible for this)

Elizabeth Gross

Politics can be a good thing, when everyone involved sticks with the rules of debate and gives all concerned a change to participate. But show me where that is happening. No, Really, if you know of a great organization that runs smoothly, let us know. Leave a comment. We can all do with some good role models.

OK, I'll stop reading the news now and go back to my biography of Liz Taylor.

(No "politics" there, heh?)

There once were pictures with the last two posts, however, I believe they were NOT free for use so some time later they disappeared. Did Word Press delete them? I don't know and I didn't ask..

Lesson Learned #4

Don't think you can get away with something when your host site is an authority on legality.

So at this point I was about a month into the blog, Still hopeful that eventually I would get readers, maybe even customers. Still riding that initial wave of creativity.

Next up, my news junkie persona kicks in.

Elizabeth Gross

Virus – Just As Bad As You Thought

The word virus is in the news again today. Nothing to do with computers, though. This one is an ancient, unknown-until-now specimen. Found in the Siberian permafrost, scientists have found that it kills amoebas. Dun-da-DUN-dun!

The news story I read, here Giant Virus Resurrected from Permafrost After 30,000 Years, says that it doesn't infect multi-cell organisms (of which humans are one). But am I paranoid in thinking that it does not say HOW they know that?

The gist of the article is that we really don't know if these long-dormant virions can bring back disease that killed Neanderthals. And that there may be other menacing contagions lurking under the melting ice and snow that the impending climate change will bring to the surface. And that It could bring about a pandemic apocalypse. Although, to be fair, according to the article, most scientists disagree.

And anyway, we're much smarter than Neanderthals.

Aren't we?

A virus is an ultra-microscopic infectious agent that replicates in the cells of living hosts, such as plants, animals, and bacteria. It can cause disease, even death.

Okay, so we know that we should protect ourselves from viral infections. Hand washing, wearing masks, eating healthy, getting exercise, and all that, will help. But if a virus wants to git 'cha, it will. They are vicious little buggers.

What can a virus infect you with? They range from the Common Cold, and Flu,to Ebola, West Nile, and HIV. Antibiotics DO NOT kill viruses. That's important to know. Don't try to get well by insisting your doctor pump you up with them. Instead, you need to get immunized every year for the flu, rest and drink fluids for a cold, and get to a doctor for anything you may suspect is really serious.

Elizabeth Gross

Also, if you have a viral infection, try to stay away from people. You do not want to be known as "the idiot that spread the flu all over the office."

Need more information? Try my sources: dictionary.com. and How Stuff Works.

And then tell me in comments what you think of this ancient disease alarm.

So now I thought it was time to start advertising my business. After all, this blog is supposed to be a marketing tool, right?

I had read a lot about how a blog can be a source of passive income. Meaning, I guess, make money by doing nothing. Except writing. And marketing the blog. And doing all kinds of things to make sure people know about the blog in the first place. Not very passive.

But I bravely started the process of showing my wares.

Elizabeth Gross

Who You Gonna Call?

Ghostwriter!

I'm ghostwriting an Ebook. This is a drastic statement for me, because as a lot of my friends know, I really want to be an author. I have many books in my head that just haven't gotten onto the paper....Yet. I have no doubt they will someday. But in the meantime, I'm ghostwriting an Ebook.

This freelancing thing I started doing is a means to an end. As I've said in another post, retirement should be a happy, leisurely time, and it's not going to be unless I bulk up my retirement income. So...here I am writing for other people.

Ghostwriting is when a writer writes a book, an article, a song, a resumé, whatever, and another person, who is not a writer, takes authorship. Lots of celebrities have their "autobiography" ghostwritten. Sometimes they give the writer credit, sometimes not. A lot of songs you think are written by the performer who sings them, aren't. Do you seriously think every word on every corporation website was written by the website owner? Think again, my friend.

Now why would anyone hire a ghostwriter? For an expert opinion, read this. It's by Denise Rutledge who has a website called Writing As A Ghost. She gives some pretty compelling reasons.

So, is ghostwriting a flat-out lie? Is it even ethical? I don't know. I don't consider it lying myself. If the guy (my client) wants to claim it as his own, it's OK by me cause, hey…I'm getting paid to do it.

If I sound mercenary, well, alright, maybe I am. But as I get older, I realize that having money is much more preferable than wanting money. So……

.I'm ghostwriting an Ebook.

Let me know if you like what I'm doing here. Are words your thing? Am I the only one? Please read this post and vote for your favorite kind of words.

That last sentence is showing some flop sweat. However, I did use an element I had learned about in my (now exhausting) research.

Link back to an earlier post to catch readers who just found your blog. To join those who were with me from the beginning. You know, the non-existent people who were hanging onto my every post.

So then, there's the recurring situation of deciding what to write about. Oh yeah, you can write about writer's block, but that seems a little…um…obvious. So in looking through resources I find the well-worn gem, "Write what you know". What do I know? Office work. Grandkids. Reading. Hmmm. Well, there's always television.

Elizabeth Gross

Sing Your Song

I'm sitting here listening to a PBS special on Bob Dylan. Lots
of different people are singing Dylan's songs. It occurs to
me that songs are a way of seeing inside a person's soul.
What he thinks, what she believes, how I feel about the
world.
Everyone has a song.

Sometimes I put music to my words when I talk. I use lyrics
to express an idea, or make a point. My kids give that "look".
You know the one. Mom, WTH? I don't care. Music is in
me.And it comes out.

Word Love

Let's see what our old friend dictionary.com has to say.

Sing: to utter words or sounds in succession with musical modulations of the voice.

Ah, no… singing is so much more than *uttering!* To sing is to throw open your throat and produce a melodic flow of thoughts. To sing is to use expression when expressing. To sing is to show your joy, your sorrow, your love.

Singing involves your whole body. You use your throat, of course, but also your shoulders, your hands, and depending on the tempo, your feet. It's a form of exercise. I think Willie Nelson said it best:

When you're singing, you're using extra muscles, and it requires a lot of exercise and breathing. You can't do that if you're a sissy. If I have any fitness advice for people, I'd tell them to sing more. It's good therapy, too.

Found on BrainyQuote.com

Singing changes your mood. Ever try to be angry and sing at the same time? The next time someone asks you yet another stupid question and you want to yell at them, sing your answer. You both might end up laughing… and singing.

Singing allays your fears. Whistling in the dark, humming on a walk at night, it's all the same. Even if you don't vocalize, you're thinking those comforting words.

Elizabeth Gross

Singing shows how much someone means to you. Praising the Creator, serenading your lover, soothing a child with a lullaby. Using your song to express love is the ultimate gift. Even if you can't carry a tune.

So let's sing! Open up your mouth and let it all out. Hey Mr. Tambourine Man, play a song for Me.

What do you have to sing about? Join the conversation in comments.

I was collecting a great stockpile of web sites to be used for resources, quotes, history and general information. But I was not using as much as I could have. These posts were okay, but had no real depth. I needed to explore further into a subject, make the post longer.

I learned about writing epic posts, which meant 1000 words instead of 400-500. It was praised as a way to grab an audience, to get noticed, to become an expert in your field. But I did not heed the advice.

Elizabeth Gross

It's Simply Complicated

I keep thinking this is a really relevant quote. But OMG, life just is not simple at all! It's hard, it's messy, it's sad. I want to shake it by its neck sometimes and demand it get better.

Simplicity. The word is almost elegant, isn't it? And if you haven't been following along, here are some thoughts about elegance.

The word simple means

1.easy to understand, deal with, use, etc

2.not elaborate or artificial; plain:

3.not ornate or luxurious; unadorned:

4.unaffected; unassuming; modest:

5.not complicated

Word Love

Sounds lovely. Too bad my life is elaborate, assuming, and quite difficult to understand at the moment. But isn't everybody's? Aside from maybe some monks on a mountain somewhere, life is complicated.

I have been looking into a simpler lifestyle. Minimalism. The desire to live with less overcame me a few months back when I cleaned out a closet. Oy vey! The stuff i keep! I told myself that I want, nay need, a way to get a grasp on my consumerism. To save money, of course, but also to clean out my life.

What does cleaning out entail? A yard sale just isn't enough. You need to get down into your soul and figure out what is useful, what is broken, what is unnecessary, and what is harmful. And then you NEED TO DO SOMETHING ABOUT IT. This…this is the rough stuff. Roll up your sleeves, put on some gloves, and dig deep into the soil of your existence.

There are some things you can get rid of right away. There are some people that you can distance yourself from. Other items on your mental agenda may take a bit of scraping to detach them, but you can do it. Start with an attitude of selfdiscovery, find out what you really want. Remember those dreams of your youth, and decide right now that you can achieve them. And then write a new chapter to your life.

Elizabeth Gross

I'm re-reading a book right now that I should have paid attention to when I first got it. <u>Simple Abundance: A Daybook</u> <u>of Comfort and Joy</u>, by Sarah Ban Breathnach. Divided into months, each with a theme, every day has a short homily related to that theme. March is dedicated to looking within yourself to find what to change. Today's thought:" You Are Not Your Appearance, But Does the Rest of the World Know That?" Good stuff.

So, how do you keep it simple? Do you live a complicated messy life? Or are you a minimalist? Let me know what works for you.

And FINALLY....a comment!

It was from my aunt but hey, take what you can get.

As you can see I started to dispense advice on how to live your life. Big mistake. This was not supposed to be my philosophy. It was supposed to be a way for customers to find me. But, as a lot of blogs, do, the subject was slowly evolving into something other than what was originally intended.

Lesson Learned # 5

It's OK to change the direction of a personal blog. A business blog should stick to business.

So now my direction was changing. I felt like the blog had taken on a life of its own.

I got back on track with the next post.

Elizabeth Gross

Are You Irish? Or Celtic?…And What's the Difference?

The word Celtic has a much bigger connotation than a

 person from Ireland. There are people with Celtic heritage all over the world. So if your family came from Ireland…yes, you are a Celt. But if you're from western France? Or northern Portugal? Yep, you may be Celtic!

And Scotland, Wales, and England? Definitely. There are six areas of Europe that are known as the Celtic Nations: Ireland, Scotland, Wales, Brittany, Cornwall, and the Isle of Man. These places have a distinct Celtic heritage, which shows up in their language, their music, their native dress, and their philosophy.

The Celtic entity dates back to the Bronze age. It was a cultural branch of the Indo-European family. They were a fierce, proud people. Warriors every one, if you asked Julius Caesar, who tried to conquer them in 51 B.C. Remember those Gauls he was trying to kill off? They were actually the Celts of France. But they did survive, along with their traditions.

Word Love

Certainly, the warrior class in ancient Celtic society was the aristocracy. The middle class were the intellectuals: Druids, poets (bards) and jurists. The lower class was made up of the laborers. .The Celtic religious beliefs were basically an earth-centered spirituality which today we call paganism. In fact, the word pagan is thought to have originally been used to describe the natives in these regions. Symbols have great meaning to them. Much of their artwork included spirals, lacework, and triskeles, a group of three.

And then, around the 5th century A.D. here comes this English monk, named Patrick, who also tried to "conquer" the Celts, by converting them to Christianity. He used various methods, such as the clover. Since it had 3 leaves, he supposedly used it to show the Trinity, which translated well since Celts incorporated triads into their religion also. And those Snakes Patrick was said to have driven out of Ireland? Those "snakes" were the pagans.

So why does St. Patrick's Day and the Irish culture get such a huge celebration today, other than say, Swedish, or Greek? Well, those Irish, you know they had a diaspora a while back and now they're everywhere. They intermingled with all the other immigrants, so nowadays, if you scratch a person with European bloodlines, you'll probably find a little bit of Celt in there somewhere.

Elizabeth Gross

I myself am Irish, Scottish, and German. But I consider myself to be mostly Celtic. How about you?

\Do You Have the Question?

Pop Culture alert! Do you know what has a 50th anniversary today? On March 30 in 1964 the most popular * quiz show on American TV debuted.

The category is: WORDS
The answer is: danger of loss, harm, or failure   Did you bet more than $1.00? Yay! You're today's winner!

It's a little used word outside of trivia affectionados. The word jeopardy brings to mind the "Perils of Pauline" heroinevictim on the train tracks. Or the small business losing to the big conglomerate. (Watched "You've Got Mail" lately?)

Elizabeth Gross

Today's word originally comes from Middle English *Jeopardie* which in turn is from the Old French *jeu parti* meaning "a divided game; an even chance." Dictionary.com says a second definition is the "danger or hazard of being found guilty."

In the sense of being an even chance at a game, it seems to me jeopardy refers to the old street games with three cups and the coin hidden under one of them. Everybody knows that you were always in jeopardy of losing that one.

And when talking about the court system, people jeopardize their life every time they choose crime over honesty.

So, in honor of my favorite TV game, I will be announcing a new venture for EJG Research in the coming weeks. It involves my leisure-time passion, trivia. You'll need to get on the mailing list to find out how you can get a free Ebook!

* not just my opinion. TV Guide ranked Jeopardy! the number one game show in 2013.

Frustration AKA Arrrgggghhhh!

Too many chocolates. Not enough stripes. And those friggin' bombs! I hate those bombs!

Yeah, you all know what I'm talking about. That all time frustration generator Candy Crush. The game we love to hate.

Elizabeth Gross

Frustration is that feeling of helpless exasperation. It causes huge sighs, clenched teeth, a furrowed brow, and pulled-out hair. A strong emotion if there ever was one.

However, it can also be a method of taking a breather from whatever it is that is troubling you. And you should actually breathe. The kind of breath that blows your bangs upwards. A good deep breath that lets you sit and think for a moment, so you aren't rushing headlong into angry.

Anger causes changes in your body. Your muscles tense, you breathing gets shorter, your seratonin levels fall, you can't think clearly. These changes can lead to heart attacks, strokes, and debilitation. If you are frustrated all the time, you can learn to use it as a method of stepping back and reevaluating the situation.

Frustration can save your life.

The word comes from *1425–75; late Middle English frustracioun < Latin frustrātiōn-* and can mean *"a feeling of dissatisfaction, often accompanied by anxiety or depression, resulting from unfulfilled needs or unresolved problems."* (dictionary.com)

Unresolved may be the key word here. When you can't do what you want, or say what you mean, or get to where you need to be, the emotion builds up. In order to fix a problem, you must resolve the situation. But when you are stopped by frustration, you may think there is just no way!

However...

That bout of frustration could be a ping from your subconscious asking you "What are you doing?" Pay attention to those pings. They are your authentic self calling out your BS. Letting you decide "What do I really want here?" "Should I continue or change it up?" "Am I being successful or just winging it?"

Or maybe it's just "Do I really want to get to level 267?"

I REALLY hate those bombs!

_____

So now I'm getting a few more comments. One every couple of posts. And I'm feeling pretty good about my content. But the business isn't getting any hits. I'm not making any money, outside of the jobs I pick up from article mills.

Now it's time to get serious. I decided to start a whole new endeavor and advertise it on my blog. The whole idea of this blog is trivia. It's one thing I am really good at. How could I convert that passion into money? And after a bit of thinking, I had it. I was going to create Trivia books.

And in order to publicize them, I went straight for the throat. Social Media. The next post was this:

EJG Research now has a page on Facebook.

https://www.facebook.com/ejgresearch

The page is devoted to trivia. If you're a trivia fan, please join in the discussions. I would love to hear from you.

I'll be running Trivia Quiz games several times a week.
Come and play!

The games never happened. I tried a few times but nobody showed up to play. But the page is still there. And getting new readers all the time.

Next up was an actual advertisement.

What Secret Ingredient Should You Use in Your Writing?

What is the reason you write? To sell? To amuse? To generate a mailing list? All of the above?

You want your readers to keep coming back to your site. Or continue to read your books. So you spend valuable time at the keyboard. Writing. Thinking. Writing. Until you come up with a great piece.

It's good. It says what you want to say. It might even bring in some income.

But is it entertaining?

If you respond "not really…." I have a solution.

It's creative, it's fun, it's educational. And it holds people's interest. Long enough to make your readers say, "This is a cool blog / website / book. I think I'll come back."

It's a resource of information that shows your readers that you think in a creative way. It adds value to your content.

And, it's easy to find…. Well…if easy means spending hours searching for just the right bit of information that matches your vision and your voice.

Elizabeth Gross

You see, just any old piece of knowledge won't do it for you. Throw in a random tidbit and people will read it, but not quite get why it's there.

So what can change readers into customers? Imagine an ebook that has a collection of trivia specific to your business.

Let's say you're a food critic. Could you use a trivia book detailing the history of famous recipes?

What if you write about travel? I bet a trivia collection about the night life in European ports sounds good.

Maybe you blog for the home school market. How about a collection on the lives of Native Americans who were elected to government positions?

Resource books of trivia, filled only with the data you require, can be a valuable addition to your reference materials. I'm working on a project that will create short, easy to digest, ebooks, each with trivia on one topic – the one YOU need.

Find out the details here.

This was another suggestions from blogging how-to sites. Create a free item to give away to people who sign up for your mailing list. Setting up a mailing list is easy. Give it a catchy name. Mine was "The Trivia Tribe." Creating the item was easy. A general trivia book explaining how you can have your very own trivia expert (me).

But if you have a tiny readership for your blog, the odds of anyone subscribing to an email list are slim to none. And none it was.

Lesson Learned #6

Using all the ideas you hear about does not necessarily equate to success.

Soon after that I went back to writing a blog.

Elizabeth Gross

Is Alchemy Real?

What do you think of when you see the word **alchemy**? Potions. Sorceresses. Wizards. Magic. Yes, fantasy uses the notion of alchemy to conjure up scenes of intrigue and mystical goings-on. But what if it's true…that we can change one thing into another? Well, don't we do that ALL THE TIME?

Have you ever poured flavored sugar into water and used it to quench someone's thirst?

Have you ever taken, milk, eggs, flour, sugar, and a little baking soda and created a whole new edible item?

Word Love

Have you ever combined vinegar and baking soda to make a powerful cleaning agent?

Well then... you are an alchemist!

The word itself goes all the way back to ancient Egypt and comes from the Arabic Al-Kemi, which is "divine chemistry." The users of alchemy were the wise ones of their culture, the scholars, the teachers, the healers. They all used minerals and plants and other natural substances to create medicines and metals and chemicals in order to heal and otherwise help their fellow man.

Out of their experiments arose new disciplines, such as chemistry, physics, mathematics, and philosophy. Science was created in those practices which society began to believe were magical and thus, to be feared. Eventually the dark ages came upon the human race and science was hidden away.

The renaissance brought it back in force and from then on we have had the benefits of the ancient healers. Alchemy brought the thinking man to the forefront of society again. Great minds like Paracelsus, Issac Newton, Francis Bacon, and Carl Jung studied alchemy to explain the world around us and who we are as human beings.

Alchemy also brought about a different way of looking at our lives. Change, as I have written about here, is a life-altering idea. To wonder what would happen if you did a certain thing in a particular way, and then do it, is a personal alchemy that you create within yourself.

For more information, you can visit The Alchemy Website by Adam McLean. It is wonderfully fascinating.

And for all you amazing readers of mine, let's go to the comments!

What's the Difference Between Retro and Vintage?

Throw back Thursdays are a recent meme going around the web. On any Thursday you're supposed to show an old picture of yourself or something else from your past. I'm not sure if you are then supposed to laugh at the old clothes and hair styles, or just commiserate with your friends that you ever looked like that.

I mentioned to my daughter that I feel like every day is throw back for me because most of my clothes are probably retro. (I hate getting rid of stuff that is still good.) And that I was planning a post on the word. And she replied, "Make sure they understand the difference between vintage and retro. It drives me crazy when people misuse those words."

Well, I couldn't deny I didn't really know the difference. Aren't the words kinda, sorta, interchangeable?

Elizabeth Gross

So, being the research nut that I am, and never one to back away from a dictionary challenge, I looked it up.

Retro means pertaining to or revived from the past. It's a shortened form of the word retroactive. So anything done in the past which has been brought back into use is retro.

Vintage refers to something old and of lasting interest or importance. It comes from the wine making culture. A bottle from a vintage year is usually very good. And expensive. It has come to mean anything that is old and worthy of remembering.

So a psychedelic print from the 1960's is retro. I can imagine wearing one today.
They're cute. But not vintage.

And a dress from the Gilded Age, circa 1890, is vintage, but not retro. If I wore something like this to work I believe my sanity would be questioned

Word Love

OK, I think I've got it. My clothes are definitely not vintage.

And no,they're not retro either.

They're just old.

Another gem I picked up from the writing sites is to use a question for the title of a post. Makes people want to know the answer.

Good advice. Still didn't work for me.

At this point it was three months into the blog. I had changed the format, changed the page appearance, changed the direction. And was no closer to a thriving business startup.

I knew intellectually that it takes a long time to get a business up and running. I wasn't worried. I had a full time job that was supporting me, so money was not an issue. Emotionally though, it's hard to sustain a mindset for working when it is not getting results.

Blogging is a lot of work. You need stamina to keep it up day after day. When you doing it for fun, it's a joy. And I was having fun. For the next several month I kept at it. But six months in, something was different.

I was getting to the age where I should be thinking about retirement. I was exploring ideas of what to do when work was not needed. (For me, this would be age 62 when Social Security kicked in.) It was reflected in my writing.

Five Senses, Why We Need Them

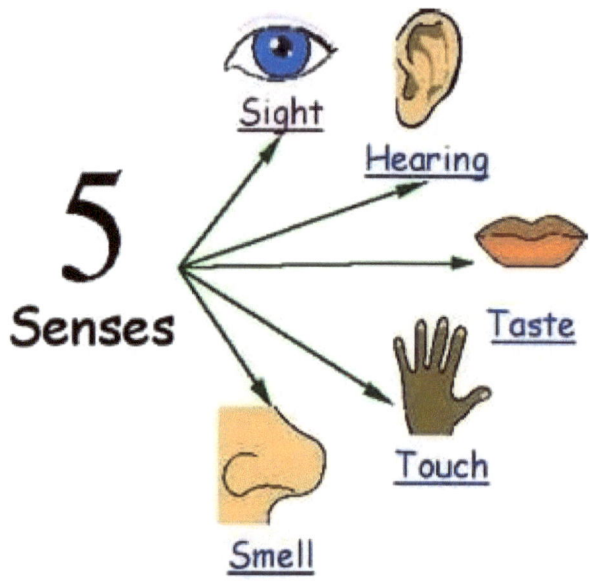

I love the smell of lilacs in the afternoon.

I love the taste of hot fudge on vanilla ice cream.

I love the feel of freshly landered sheets.

I love the sound of my grandaughter's laughter.

I love the sight of a sunrise after an overnight thunderstorm.

Our senses are the way we experience the world. They are essential for making sense of our surroundings. We sense a change in our life when something is not going the same way it was yesterday.

The word "sense" has many meanings, and there are many ways of using it. The definition depends on what is said.

(from dictionary.com)

1. any of the faculties, as sight, hearing, smell, taste, or touch, by which humans and animals perceive stimuli originating from outside or inside the body.

2. these faculties collectively.

3. their operation or function; sensation.

4. a feeling or perception produced through the organs of touch, taste, etc., or resulting from a particular condition of some part of the body: to have a sense of cold.

5. a faculty or function of the mind analogous to sensation: the moral sense.

What would happen if you lost one of your senses? If you have all of them now, this may be hard to imagine. If you have lost one or more, you may already know how to compensate.

I find it hard to decide which sense would be the most difficult to live without. Sight, of course, is crucial to my job. Taste and smell I think would be easier to loose than the others. Being 60 years old, I already have lost these to a degree. Touch would be sad

Word Love

because I have small grandchildren (one an infant) that I love to cuddle with. And hearing would devastate me because I love music.

Let's celebrate the fact that we can sense things in our world.

Elizabeth Gross

Reflection is More Than A Face In a Mirror

"Out on the road today,
I saw a Deadhead sticker on a Cadillac.
A little voice inside my head said Don't look back
You can never look back."
Don Henley

If you are of a certain age, like me, you know what this song is talking about. You can't go back to your youth. Everything changes – love, career, family. It's hard to see the future at 20. And harder yet to remember all the plans that were never fulfilled at 60.

The word **reflection** means looking at something with thoughtful consideration. As I look back on my life, I see many things that were good, some that were great, and of course, some that were mistakes.

Am I thoughtful when thinking about them? Not always. Amused, sad, bitter, angry, and I guess, sometimes thoughtful. Usually the bad stuff doesn't even get considered. (Forgetfulness in aging can be a good thing, hehe)

My career path changed several times. I started out to be a nurse, switched to librarian, and ended up as an receptionist at a senior housing community.

I've been married twice. Divorced. Widowed. Raised kids. Lost parents. Gained gandchildren.

I wasn't a deadhead, but my kids call me an old hippie.

A fairly normal life actually. Not too much that I would call bad. At least, nothing I would talk about.

Isn't it true that everyone has things in their life that are not to be talked about?

I'm approaching a landmark birthday…60! Woah! When did that happen? **Reflection** is an exercise that I really should do more often. Especially since I'm calling myself a writer these days. It's good for the soul, so they tell me.

Elizabeth Gross

Why all this **reflection**? I've been thinking seriously about retirement lately. I need to get my life in line so I can take off one of these days. So considering what I've done (so far) and what I might do is my way of re-setting the mind. I'm ready mentally, but not financially. Waitin' for that Social Security to kick in.

How much reflection is worthwhile? Does thinking about the meaning of life make your head hurt? If you have any suggestions about retirement, if you were a deadhead, if you're having a birthday, leave a comment. All ideas are welcome here.

Word Love

And by the time the end of the summer came around, I was ready to quit. I was posting once a week, if that. It wasn't because of a lack of ideas. There were still plenty of those. I had run out of desire. And this post sums it up nicely.

Elizabeth Gross

Wanderlust: A romantic notion or a way of life?

A strong desire to travel. A love of the open road. A yearning to get up and go. All these phrases describe a word that comes from Middle High German. *Wandern* (to hike) and *Lust* (desire) eventually were loosely translated into English as "enjoyment of roaming about."

"Got to find my corner of the sky" Schwartz

The idea of a wanderer has become ingrained in the American way of life. So many songs, poems, movies and books are about wanderers that many non-Americans think no one here ever stays in one place for long. And it's true that in the past decade or so, people who live in one location, or work at one job for years have started being looked at as novelties.

But is this a good thing? Or just another national growth phase? I suppose time will tell. Cities are always growing or shrinking, roads are built and roads disappear. Schools are hard pressed to keep up with the ever-changing landscapes. Maybe the United States just wasn't meant to be laden with history of place.

"Not all those that wander are lost" Tolkein

I have had wanderlust in my soul my whole life. I believe it was embedded in my psyche by my father. He took the family on Sunday drives and cross-country vacations. He didn't mind when we got lost out in the country. (I really think he secretly enjoyed it) He taught me how to read maps, and encouraged me to study the National Geographic ones. I grew up with the idea that exploring was a desirable way to spend time.

As I got older, life got in the way of my wandering habit. Didn't have time or the money to do much traveling. Occasionally there would be a vacation trip to visit family.

Elizabeth Gross

After the kids were grown, my husband and i spent many Sunday afternoons diving through the country surrounding our city. However due to financial and health reasons, we never traveled for pleasure.

"I just can't wait to get on the road again" Nelson

But now, nearing the end of my working life, I find the thought of following the road to wherever it leads is a doable thing. The song of Bilbo Baggins "The Road Goes Ever, Ever On" is my new motto. I want to buy a motorhome, and live in it as i travel the land. I'm seriously deciding to become a RV fulltimer when the Social Security kicks in. Fortunately, Wi-Fi is available wherever you go, so writing will continue to be a source of income.

How many of you are wanderers, either part-time or fulltime?

Any advice for me?

So there you have it. My journey into and out of the world of blogging for business. I have had other blogs and will again, I'm sure. But this one was a disappointment in that I couldn't get what I wanted out of it.

I hope you have more success than I did.

Here's some final insight into why I began..

Elizabeth Gross

Research – Why Do We Do It?

If we knew what it was we were doing, it would not be called research, would it?

~ Albert Einstein

The definition of the word research gives no clue at all of what a satisfying pastime it can be.

diligent and systematic inquiry or investigation into a subject in order to discover or revise facts, theories, applications, etc.

I've loved research my whole life. I can remember reading books at a very young age and wondering what it would be like to live in the time or place in the book. I wanted to know about them. The people, the places, the culture (even before I knew what that word meant).

I had quite an active imagination (if I do say so myself) and would act out the stories. I was Pippi Longstocking having glorious adventures. I was Jo in Little Women yearning to be a writer. I traveled across the plains with Ma and Pa Ingalls. The library was absolutely my favorite place.

I learned about the encyclopedia and how it answered my questions. But even better, it created more! Questions. Answers. Learning became an addiction. I began to understand that the world was a much larger place than my neighborhood. People were far more interesting because they were not all like me.

I would read anything. My brother tells people that I would read a Ketchup bottle if I couldn't have a book at the dinner table. I once received a cookbook for Christmas and spent the day reading it. My cousins thought I was bonkers.

I don't think I can fully explain how much I love to read. I will read, literally, anything. I collect pamphlets on vacation. I have a Kindle app on my phone. Wikipedia is the first thing I bookmark when i get a new computer. I can't throw away my junk mail without reading it!

But I learn…so much. Sometimes I think my brain will overload. But it won't. Finding out what we don't know expands the capacity of the brain. The more stuff we put in, the bigger the storage space gets. Brilliant!

And all that reading led me here. To a business based on research. To a blog about words. And the joy of being able to dispense knowledge to you, my lovely readers. For that is what research is really all about. Learning new things so you can teach others.

What were your favorite books as a child? And did they create a thirst for research?

ABOUT THE AUTHOR

Elizabeth Gross is a freelance content provider, author, and lover of trivia. She has started a series of children's trivia books and is putting together a novel. She is available to hire through her business EJG Research. via her website www.ejgresearch.com.

Elizabeth works for a not-for-profit senior housing community until her anticipated retirement in 2016. She lives in Fort Wayne, Indiana.